# God's Miracle
(And My New Truck)

By Peyton A. Langford

ISBN-10: 1477515585
ISBN-13: 978-1477515587

# TABLE OF CONTENTS

# FOREWARD

Let me just start out by saying that I'm not a writer and this may not turn out too well. But God gave me this story to tell and I'm going to try my best to tell it. You will notice that I have a tendency to write like I talk, so this story may ramble a bit. I have been told that I ramble off on too many tangents when I try to tell something. Sooo- let me go on and apologize for that to start with.

It really doesn't matter who I am, but I guess that I will tell you a little bit about myself. My name is Peyton Langford. I am 49 years old, married, with 2 children. My wife and I have been married for, well since 1988. (I hate trying to do math in my head, so I'll just state the year.) My wife's name is Irene and we have two daughters: Jessica and Lindsey. Jessica is 15 and Lindsey is 12. I am very proud of my family. They all pitch in to help me on the farm. Like I said, I am not a writer, what I am, is a farmer. I farm outside of the little town of Autaugaville, AL. I'm not the best farmer in the world; I'm probably not the best at anything. I'm surely not the best Christian, not even a very good one. That's why writing this doesn't seem like something that I would do.

When you're reading this, please don't quit because it seems to be going nowhere. I could tell that almost everyone that I told this story to, about middle ways, thought that, and some even said that, "this really is taking a long time". It rambles around and around but, at the end, it comes together in such a way that it absolutely astonished me. (I know that "astonished" is a really big word that I never use; but, I couldn't think of any other word that really described how astonishing that this ordeal was.)

This whole story is about me getting a new, well new to me, truck and the circumstances that surrounded the purchase. When it was over, I knew that God had performed a miracle in my life (not the first one that I have received) and provided me with the truck that I had really wanted. It wasn't until a couple of days later that I realized that it may not have been all about me getting the truck, but about me getting the story. I have tried to tell everyone that I see, but I hope by writing this story, it will reach many more people than I would have come in contact with. I hope that it will have as biga' (I told you that I write like I talk.) impact on your life as it has mine.

# I-MY PLAN

This whole story started as I was pulling a tractor to Dothan, AL. with my 2003 one ton, crew cab, four-wheel drive Chevrolet truck. The truck was trying to run hot and the engine started making a funny knocking noise. I had to unhook from the thirty-six ft. gooseneck trailer and leave my tractor and trailer sitting in a parking lot on the side of Hwy 231, outside of Montgomery. I didn't have another truck that would have made it that far, and the only one that I thought would have, just tore up. I left the tractor there in the Trailer World parking lot overnight and started looking for me another truck the next morning, after making a few phone calls and finding out that a remanufactured Durimax engine for the Chevrolet was eleven thousand dollars.

My wife and I had met a man at an equipment auction a few weeks earlier that had told us that he owned a car dealership in Mississippi, and that he always had some one ton trucks, if we ever needed one. I called him that morning and he had what I thought was just perfect for me, a 2008 crew cab, four wheel drive Ford 450. That was a larger truck than my one ton and I always have liked great big stuff. (A friend of mine tells me that I like to buy great big stuff because I compensate for the fact that I have always been kinda skinny.) I told the guy that that was just what I was looking for and that I would head that way. Me and my wife and our two daughters headed to Mississippi and bought me that Ford. I didn't know anything about the new Fords, I just knew that it was a big honkin' truck and that was exactly what I needed. We all took it for a test drive and it did great, except that it pulled a little to the right. I could get it aligned and that would be fine. He was giving a really great deal on the truck. All that I needed to do to it was put a flat-bed on it. (I work better out of a flat-bed truck than one with the dually bed. I can't reach over the fenders to get stuff out of the bed, and I need an air compressor and tool boxes. I'll stop there, but I can come up with a million reasons why I need one.) I also need me a big ol' bumper and a winch. (I could come up with a million reasons for these items too.) I was tickled with the truck, even though it had roll-up windows instead of power; and we headed home with it that night.

The next morning I left early, hooked to my trailer that was still in the parking lot, and made it to Dothan without a hitch. Man, that truck did great. That thing pulled better than any truck that I had ever owned. It rode good and had plenty of power, although I noticed that I had to fill up with fuel way too fast. That thing got eight and a half miles per gallon! With fuel prices steadily going up, I had a feeling that I had bit off more than I could chew. My wife even got mad with me every time that I went to town if I went in my truck. She made me drive her car because it got better gas mileage. I'm a farmer; I don't want to drive up to a tractor dealership to get parts in a little black car. I'm dressed like a farmer, all nasty and greasy, but driving a little car. It's bad when the parts guy asks you if you've got some mudgrips for that thing. Then to make matters worse, I would have to tell him that my wife would not let me drive my truck because it used too much fuel.

It was becoming increasingly apparent that I was going to have to get rid of this truck. I tried not to think about it and make it the truck of my dreams. I found me a big ol' bumper and a fifteen thousand pound winch, had them installed and started looking for a flat-bed. I quickly realized that new flat-beds were really pricey. I decided to hold off on that one for a while. I did buy me a new air compressor that I just sat in the bed of the truck on a pallet. It didn't look that great, but it was functional. I also put me a used chrome checker-plate tool box across the bed behind the compressor. It rubbed all the paint off the new compressor but it didn't tare up nothing. (I told you that I write like I talk.) After all this, I was fairly happy with the truck, even though I had to ask permission to drive it very far.

One day I was up in the pasture checking on the cows and I stopped to look at one of them. When I tried to pull off, I noticed that I wasn't moving. I was just sitting still. I was sitting on a little incline, but not anything steep. My back tires were just sitting there spinning in a patch of clover. Realizing that I was stuck in a patch of clover, it was now also evident that my dream truck lacked a limited slip differential. (Another option that I feel as though I can't live without.) After close inspection of the tires that had been feverishly spinning and not moving the truck even one inch, I also noticed that the tires didn't really have as much tread on them as I had thought. I called around and a set of tires would run somewhere around two thousand dollars.

I now knew that the big honkin' truck that I had once thought was perfect, would have to go.

If any of yall ever have to sell a big fuel guzzling truck when fuel prices are around four dollars a gallon, I hope yall have better luck than I did. My truck ad ran for several months without a single phone call from a prospective buyer. After careful consideration, I figured that I must have been asking too much for my truck. The Kelly Blue Book valued it at around thirty-six thousand dollars, even though I didn't pay but twenty-five thousand. I thought that I had gotten a great deal on the truck, but evidently people knew way more than I did about these trucks. I had started out at twenty-nine thousand dollars with the bumper and winch or twenty-seven thousand without them. (For some reason I thought that I could make some money on this thing. I was wrong.) I dropped the price to twenty-six thousand dollars including the bumper and the winch, because I remembered that I was still going to have to spend two thousand on a set of tires if I kept driving the truck.

I had two phone calls within two days of the new price coming out. The first guy said that he wanted the truck and after giving him the VIN number over the phone, where he could apply for his loan, I waited for his follow-up call. He still hasn't called me back. The second guy came out and looked at the truck. He was as excited about it as I was when I first looked at it. He wanted it. He wrote down the VIN number and went back to Montgomery to get the money. He never called back. I don't know what happened to these two, but evidently they checked on this type truck before buying. Something that I never did.

About every seven years or so, I get the feeling that I would like to start some other type of business. (This really does have something to do with this story. It's not just another tangent that my wife says that I get on in the middle of my conversations. It really will play a part, I promise. Just bare with me.) Most every type business that I have been in is the type that causes me to do some type work: you know, physical or time consuming work. Along with farming, which I have always been in since graduating college, my wife an I were in the fresh water lobster business for about seven years and we were also in the guided pheasant, chucker and quail business for about seven years. We now, along with farming, have been in the guided deer, turkey and dove hunting business for about sixteen years. The new type business that I want to start is one that I could have and not have to do manual labor. I have been thinking of maybe some type of consulting work. I could get paid for just showing up and telling folks how I would do stuff. Man, that would be great, getting paid for my time and expertise. Too bad I'm probably not an expert at anything; although I have made a lot of mistakes in my life and could tell people how not to do stuff. I'm kinda like an older fellow named Cecil once told me, "I'm not completely useless, I can always be used as a bad example". Be that as it may, I am trying to start a consulting business in the wildlife management field. My Agronomy degree, twenty-eight years in farming and the sixteen years in the hunting business, I hope, makes me somewhat knowledgeable of how to manage land and wildlife resources on property owned by individuals that have bought the land for recreation. (Now that I have finished my commercial, I will try and tie it back to the story.)

One of our deer hunters this year had asked me to come to Scottsboro and look at some of his land. We had made plans two or three times but his schedule never worked out for him to have time for me to come up. Right prior to one of the times I was to drive up to Scottsboro, I received a phone call from a fellow from Harpersville. He had been traveling somewhere and picked up a copy of The Bulletin Board, the little ad paper that my truck was in. They don't have that paper in Harpersville. He liked the look of my truck, (He said it was a good looking truck.) and said that he would be interested in it. I informed him that I was going to be in north Alabama the next week and we could meet for him to see the truck on my way up to Scottsboro. (This way, I could drive my truck instead of my wife's car. This was going to work out perfect.) Well, the hunter called and had to cancel our meeting again, so I didn't carry the truck to get it looked at. I kept waiting for the hunter to call and reschedule, but he never did. About a week and a half later the truck guy called me back. He still wanted the truck and wanted to see when I was coming to north Alabama.

Not wanting to miss this opportunity for a possible sale, I told him that I would bring the truck up there in the next couple of days. He told me that he really wanted it and if I could bring the truck up there, then we could carry it by the credit union and have them look at it and see if they would give him the money. I started cleaning the truck up that day. The tool box came out of the bed, the air compressor came off and the new bed liner went down. (The dealer in Mississippi had put in the bed liner to cover all the dents and missing paint in the bed. I did the same thing.) I washed that thing, waxed it, (I hadn't waxed a vehicle in twenty-five years.) cleaned all the interior and ArmorAlled the dash and even the running boards and the rearview mirrors. Man, that thing was beautiful!

I finished cleaning and polishing it on a Tuesday morning. (It took me two full days and that morning.) I called the fellow and told him that I was on my way.

The guy had a fruit stand on the side of US Hwy 280 and I was to meet him there. I finally found the fruit stand and pulled in. The fellow was there. He was an older gentleman, had a pretty good limp and walked with a cane. He had told me that he had been diagnosed with prostate cancer in 2008 and that he was in bad shape on the phone. I kinda considered this to be a sign because I had been told that I could have prostate cancer the week prior, due to my PSA test. (I was tested twice over several days and my number was too high the first time and higher the second time. I was really worried and I thought that I might could, maybe, ask this fellow how it felt and if there were any symptoms that I should be looking for. My urologist had put me on antibiotics for two weeks and then I was to take the test over. If the number was still too high, he was going to have to do the biopsy. I took microbiology in college and have always been afraid of a biopsy. I think that if you go in there and tear pieces off, and it is cancer, that on a cellular level, that you can't help but send cancer cells running through your blood stream. You know that it can't cut perfectly and is bound to tear some cells a loose and they are now a loose in your body. I'm sure that I can be proved wrong, but that's just the way that I feel and that biopsy deal scared me to death.)

He looked at my truck for just a few minutes and we got in it for him to take his test drive. I didn't have a clue where we were going; I was just trying to get up the nerve to ask him about prostate cancer. Like I said, I thought this was a way that God had of helping me deal with the fact that I may have it also. I was thankful that He was going to let me talk to this man. (I have a friend of mine that I used to pick cotton for that has prostate cancer, but I didn't want to ask him because I didn't want everyone in the community to know that I might have it. This was perfect because nobody knew this guy and he could tell me without anyone knowing it.) I never got up the nerve and we got to talking about the truck and how good it looked and about it pulling to the right. I told him that it had done that ever since I had it and that I meant to get it aligned, but I had never had it done.

After a few minutes, to my surprise, we arrived at the credit union. We walked in and he told the girl that he was there to get some money to buy my truck. (I was really glad that I had decided to carry the title, just in case.) The process went really well. Then, for some reason, it hit a road block. The lady that was helping us was having some type problem with the computer and then she got up and left. She finally came back and said that there was a problem with the VIN number. She had me to read it to her to make sure that she had copied it down correctly. Since I'm old now and had forgotten and left my reading glasses in the truck, I had to borrow the fellow's glasses to read it to her; but we finally figured out that she had it right to start with. For some reason, my VIN would not pull up on NADA. (I was worried that this was why no one ever called me back that had previously wanted this truck. Surely it wasn't stolen or anything like that. I even wondered if that guy in Mississippi had altered the VIN and maybe it was a truck that had been totaled out before and was rebuilt under another VIN. I could see this sale falling apart any second now. I could be stuck with this truck forever, or the police may even come get it.)

Finally the lady told me that the problem was that their NADA program did not cover anything larger than a 350; it didn't have any information on a 450. I told her to try Kelly Blue Book because that is where I had found it. Her boss told her to call a dealership and ask them to value the truck. (This also scared me to death because I worried that they would say that the truck was worth less than I was asking. I could see this deal still going up in smoke!) All she got at the dealership was a recording of someone's voicemail. The man made the statement that it didn't look like my truck wanted to be sold. She called back and finally got a real person to answer. They had a program to find the value and they would do it for her, while she answered the questions. They would ask her a question like: "what is the VIN, what options and what is the mileage." She, in turn, would ask me, I would tell her and she would tell them.

As I told her what the mileage was, the man asked, "How many miles did you say?" I repeated ninety-six thousand three hundred I think. The lady had finished her conversation and was going to wait on the dealership to fax her over the results when the man said, in a somewhat louder voice, "I didn't know that it had that many miles. If I had known that, I don't think I would have wanted it." He went on to say that when he heard the mileage, that the number hit him right in between the eyes like a ton of bricks. He said that he kinda wanted to just forget the whole thing! I tried to explain to him that I thought that we had talked about the mileage because I had told him that the reason it had so many miles is that the environmental company that had leased the truck for the first two years had driven the truck almost everyday, all day long. He said that he didn't remember me ever telling him about the mileage and that he thought that it probably had about sixty-five or seventy thousand. He didn't know if he wanted it if it had ninety-six thousand miles. I reluctantly told him that if he didn't want it, I would just take it on back home. (Now I really saw the deal falling apart, and I thought for a fact that I had only come up there to ask him about having cancer.)

Then I remembered what the old man (Now that I'm getting a little ill with him, I'll start calling him that.) had said when the lady asked how much money he needed. He said he needed twenty-six thousand, but then turned to me and asked if it would be OK to just go on and tell her an even twenty-five thousand. I had kinda laughed it off the first time, but now I figured that is what it would take to seal this deal. I, now, somewhat more reluctantly, told him that since he didn't like that the truck had so many miles on it, that I would lower the price to twenty-five thousand. He didn't say anything for a few minutes, while me and the lady (I know that I'm supposed to put "the lady and I", but I told you that I write like I talk, and I would have said "me and the lady", so that's what I wrote.) just stared at each other and at him. He finally said that he felt bad that I had brought the truck that far and that he had made the lady "do all that work", so he figured that he would just take the truck anyway. (I wondered if he had planned that the whole time.)

By now, we had been in her office for over an hour and a half. The fax had arrived and evidently, they could loan him that amount. Things had sped up just a little bit and it looked as though we were maybe going to get this done. She had finished the title application and we were waiting for the paperwork. The old man was getting real fidgety. He kept having to move around and was making some groaning noises every now and then. He finally told us that he needed to wrap this up pretty quick because it was hard for him to sit still very long, due to the pain in his back. I wondered if the cancer caused the pain; then I remembered that he told me that he had once been run over by a truck. I turned to him and asked, "So you were run over by a truck?" (I wanted to make some type of conversation due to the fact that the mood had become very tense ever since the matter of the mileage.)

He perked up a little and explained to me that he was working for the city of Harpersville, running a backhoe, when he was run over by an eighteen wheeler. The lady also perked up and said that she remembered when it was because back then, accident victims were hardly ever air-lifted, but she remembered that he was. He went on to tell us about all his injuries. All his ribs were broken, his left femur was crushed and had to be replaced with a rod, and his back was broken in three places. I can't remember the rest of his injuries, but they were numerous. I think he said that he died several times on the table, but that every time, he came back. None of the doctors expected him to live, but he did. He didn't know how he lived or why, but that it must not have been his time. He said, "Just like with the cancer, I thought I wouldn't make it, but I did. God must have a purpose for me," he said.

The paperwork arrived and we all thought that this fiasco was almost over. I noticed that the lady was looking at something on the title application and not really saying anything. She finally said that she had made a mistake on the name and that she was going to have to delete that application and file another one. (It's been over two hours now and I am ready to get out of this place.) After waiting another fifteen minutes or so, the old man (I'm still calling him that because, even though I feel a little sorry for him now, I'm still a little ill.) asks if it would be all right if we left and he would come back the next day to sign his papers. They (By now, several people had gotten involved.) told him that would be fine and that they would go on and print me out a check. They printed me out a check, but it went to a printer in the town that the first lady had worked at before. The credit union had changed the branch that she was working at, but had not changed her code, so the check went to her old office. (By now, I have forgotten about asking the old man about having cancer.)

I finally get the check in my hand and we are out the door!

The old man had been trying to call someone on the phone ever since I met him at the fruit stand, to no avail. As we leave the credit union, we go looking for the person that he has been trying to call on the phone. It was his son. He is going to get his son to carry me back home, since I no longer have a truck to drive. We finally go to one of his son's houses, where this son, the one that is to drive me home, is working. He is building a barn/house for his brother.

We enter the soon to be barn and home combination and find the son and his employee diligently working. He was, what I would say, not real happy about the prospect of having to take me home. The old man (I stay ill a long time.) tells the son that he is just too tired, after the long ordeal at the credit union, or he would carry me himself. The son tries to tell his help what to do the rest of the evening and we all load up in, what is now, the old man's truck.

The son is driving and I am riding shotgun. We are to drop the old man off at the fruit stand and then pick up the son's four year old twin daughters from daycare. He was to pick them up that day, and since his wife was still at work, the twins have nowhere to go, so, they will have to ride with us. The son is, to say the least, perturbed.

As we drop the old man off at the fruit stand, his door has not even slammed shut when the son says to me, "This is the stupidest thing he has ever done." (That meant buying my truck.) "He doesn't have any use for this thing", he said. "It will just sit in his yard just like the other one that he has. He never runs it and every time that you try to crank it, something is wrong with it. It just sits up too much. I don't know why he buys these things. He doesn't need them, he just buys them."

I didn't know what to say, so I was really glad that we were already arriving at daycare. While he was gone, I called my wife and told her that I was now riding in someone else's truck. Before we could discuss much about the deal, the son returned with two little blonde-headed girls.

The mood kinda changed after the girls got in the truck, and after stopping to fill up with fuel, (I only put half a tank in it before I left. Just in case I did sell it, I didn't want to sell it with it full of fuel.) we headed back to Autaugaville to drop me off. I was soooo ready to be home.

Everything went fine the rest of the trip and the truck even got about fourteen and a half miles per gallon; way better than it would have if

I had been driving. I got dropped off without a hitch and the son even let the twins feed our little calf that we were bottle-feeding. He even took a picture of them to send to his wife, who was texting him to find out where they were. (Maybe he wasn't as mad with me anymore. I hoped not.)

Before he left, I gave him a business card with my cell number written on the back. He had never been here before and we had come the "back way" out of Clanton, and there were a bunch of turns that he was going to have to remember to get back to the interstate.

About five minutes after he had left, my cell phone rang. He and the girls had missed their first turn. I told him how to get back right and never heard from them again. So, I assumed that they had made it back fine the rest of the way.

I finished cleaning up the mess that I had made that morning, while washing and waxing the truck, and went on in the house to wait for Irene and the girls to make it home from town; hopeful that they would bring something good for supper. (We live out in the country and we eat supper at night. We eat dinner in the middle of the day. We have breakfast, dinner and then supper. It has always been like that for me and I refuse to call my evening meal dinner. I'm kinda funny about stuff like that.)

While I was waiting on them to come home, I sat down at the computer and commenced to try to find me a truck. There were five hundred and thirty something Dodge 3500s on eBay. I picked out about fifteen to go on my "watch list".

My family got home with a "five dollar" pizza and so I had to stop my eBayin' to eat. I gulped down my share of the pizza and got right back on the computer. That twenty-five thousand dollar check was burning a hole in my pocket and I wanted me a truck by the next day. (The real reason that I had to buy a truck quickly is that I knew that if I deposited the check in the bank, without buying a truck right away, that I would spend that money on something else, little by little, and then not have enough money left to buy me another truck. And, because I was "forced" to lower the price on my other truck, I was already short of what I had planned.) I found a couple of what I thought were "just what I needed" trucks, but none of the owners of them, which were mostly second rate dealerships that you would find on a small corner lot where a grocery store used to be, could tell me if their trucks had limited slip differentials. One of the ladies that I talked to informed me that four-wheel drive trucks didn't come with limited slip differentials; that option was only available on two-wheel drive models. (I decided right quick that I didn't want to buy anything from her.) I did find one truck in Virginia that I kinda wanted. I decided that I may ride up there and look at it. (It was just what I wanted except that it didn't have a big bumper and winch and it had a regular bed; but surely I could replace all that sometime or another. The important thing is that I would have me a truck.)

# II-GOD'S PLAN

That night I didn't sleep worth a flip! I couldn't decide what truck I really wanted and I was still waiting on my urologist to call about the test results on the possibility of me having cancer. (I had called his office two days prior and the nurse had told me that he had received the results, but that he had not looked at them. She assured me that as quick as he looked at them, that he would call me. Since it had been two full days and he hadn't called, I figured that I must have it and that he was trying to line up the biopsy before contacting me. It wasn't a very good night.) While I was laying there, not sleeping, the thought came to me that maybe I might ought to ask God for a little help in picking out a truck this time. The last time I really didn't think about it. (I'm really bad about doing things myself. It's kinda like I say, "Don't worry about it God, I got this." Then I handle the situation right quick and head directly for eminent disaster. I don't really know how to describe what it sounds like when God speaks to me, but I just hear it. It's like it just comes to me; not like my thoughts, but it's just there.) So, after asking Him for some advice, I went to the kitchen to get me something to drink. (Sometimes if I get up and get me something to drink, it kinda takes my mind off my thoughts and when I lay back down, I can go to sleep.) After laying back down, I thought about where I bought a truck one time in Tallassee: Ben

Atkinson Motors. (I always liked them up there because as long as I have known about them, it has been the same people there. The same guys have been there for I know at least 20 years and every time I take a vehicle up there, they all still know who I am. Their service department has always been great to me and I recommend them to everybody. You would have thought that I would have thought of them by myself, but I didn't.) I thanked God for the idea and decided the next morning, before leaving for Virginia, that I would call Buddy. He is the guy that I think is in charge of the truck shop, although I'm not really sure. I just know that he is the one that I always ask for.

I called Buddy the next morning around nine o'clock. (This was Wednesday; I had sold my other truck the day before on Tuesday.) He was cordial as ever and seemed to have all the time in the world to talk to me. (Buddy is one of the main reasons for me ever buying more than one vehicle from that dealership.) I asked him a million questions about the Dodge engines, transmissions, rear ends and every other thing that I could think of. (Something that I did not do when I went off "half cocked" and bought that Ford.) He told me about what engine that they have the least amount of trouble with, the transmission that holds up the longest and what type service is needed on the new trucks. While I was talking with Buddy, I threw away all the write-ups of the trucks that I had gotten off of eBay. None of the ones that I was looking at were one of the "good ones". I was about to thank him for his time and expert advice when he interrupted me and said, "Hold on, let me call a fellow and see if he still has his truck. I know a guy that has a truck just like you are looking for." He explained to me that a fellow, which he described as a real honest straight-up guy, had a one ton, crew cab, four-wheel drive Dodge that they had put a brand new motor in only a few months before. The guy that owned the truck had even let Buddy borrow the truck to try it out for a while to make sure everything was all right with the new motor. Buddy said that he had pulled hay with the truck and that he thought everything on the truck was good and that the guy had always taken real good care of the truck. Dodge had paid for most of the new motor, even though the truck was out of warranty. He didn't know how the guy (He called him Mr. Chisholm) had swung that, but he had. Buddy said that he had also replaced the clutch with a better one and put new belts and emergency brake shoes and a new water pump on the truck while they had it in the shop. He said that the bill for the truck was a little over twenty thousand dollars. (It was like a brand new truck!) Mr. Chisholm was downsizing and had told Buddy that he would be interested in selling the truck. Buddy said that he himself would have bought the truck, if he had had the money. He would call the guy and see if he still had the truck and he would have the guy call me. (I thanked Buddy and then I thanked God.)

About an hour later I received a message from Buddy that he had left two messages with the fellow that owned the truck, but that he hadn't heard from him. About thirty minutes after that, Mr. Chisholm called me. He was a real nice guy and we talked for about forty minutes, about the truck and everything else. (My wife tells me that I talk too much.) I finally got around to asking him what he wanted for the truck and he told me that he would take twenty-three thousand. (That was two thousand dollars less than I got for my truck and only three thousand dollars more than the bill was for redoing his truck in the shop. I was tickled to death!) I asked him if I could come look at the truck that day and he said that that would be fine. He owned a frame and body shop and they were fixin' to leave to go to lunch, but that they would be back in about forty-five minutes and would be there all afternoon. I told him that I would call him and tell him when I left to head that way. It was about, I don't know, maybe, forty miles to Slapout. (That's really the name of the town where the truck was; I promise I didn't make that up.)

I called Stan, a buddy of mine, (He's the one that thinks I buy "great big" stuff to compensate for my skinny frame size.) to see if he would go with me. (Stan is without a doubt my best friend. His dad and I were good friends and his dad was my first partner in the deer hunting business. His dad's name was Stanford. He was killed in 1998 by a drunk driver. He and his wife were coming home from seeing a friend in the hospital and were only three miles from home when they were struck head on by a drunk driver that had decided to pass in a no passing zone. The drunk was running about one hundred and ten miles per hour when he hit them. This was the drunk driver's third DUI that year! I still don't know how he was still on the road. Stanford was killed and Ms. Sara was bummed up real bad and had a broken pelvis. Stanford was the kind of guy that you were tickled to death to see if you were having any kind of trouble. He could fix anything and was eager to help anyone in need. There was even a man at Stanford's funeral that spoke that didn't even know Stanford but Stanford had found him broke down on the side of the road. Stanford looked at the man's truck, figured out what was wrong with it, carried the man to town to get the parts, brought the man back to his truck and put the parts on his truck and sent the man on his way. Stanford didn't charge the man a dime. (I hope folks speak that well of me when I'm gone.) Stan said he would go if we could stop and pick up some lunch. (Me and Stan always seem to have to go to town around lunch time. Go figure.) We headed toward town, deposited my twenty-five thousand dollar check at the bank and went to eat at the Cracker Barrel. When we left there, I called Mr. Chisholm and told him that we were on our way.

As we were pulling out into the road, my phone rang. It was my urologist. I really didn't want to get this call right now; my day was going too good. The nurse told me to hold on and the doctor would speak to me in just a second. (A lot of things go though your mind during those six seconds that you are waiting for the doctor to get on the phone. The only thing that I remember though, is having just enough time to ask God one more time for me not to have cancer.) The doctor came on the phone and in a normal (Almost too normal, but I guess he does this every day.) tone of voice said, (You know, it just hit me that if I was writing a script for a soap opera, that this would be the perfect time for a commercial break. Hee. Hee. Just a little humor to lighten the mood.) "Peyton your numbers are down and I think that you will be fine." You know, I very seldom say "Thank You Lord" out loud but I said it and probably really meant it more than any time before. (The way that I found out that there may have been a problem with my PSA test results was that I took a blood test to try and get some additional life insurance. I had never been very concerned about having much life insurance because I didn't think that I needed it. I had a good deal of bank stock that I was planning on selling when I got ready to retire and I figured that if I died, that my wife and kids could live off of that. That seemed like a great idea until the stock dropped from thirty-six dollars a share to around a dollar and twenty cents. All of a sudden I had no retirement, and nothing for my kids and my wife to live on if something happened to me. I don't know if they can make a living on the farm without me and if they couldn't, they would have to sell the farm that has been in my family since 1943 and they would have to have living expenses until it sold. I felt as though I had failed them and if something had happened to me, they, as they struggled to pay bills, may have considered me to have failed them also. I think the prospect of that was way worse than the fact that I might die from cancer.)

I felt like the weight of the whole world had been lifted off my shoulders. I wasn't worried about the cancer any more; and now, maybe, I would have a chance to get some insurance. And, I'm going to look at the truck that I believe that God has picked for me. (It's a really good day.)

As we drove toward Slapout to see the truck, I called my wife to tell her the good news. I acted like it was no big deal, even though I had been worried sick. She acted like it too, like she wasn't upset, but I could tell she had started to cry as she was hanging up the phone.

When me and Stan arrived at the guy's shop, I could see the white Dodge sitting out beside it. It looked great. It even had a big bumper and a winch. (Thank You Lord!) We all talked about the truck for a while and me and Stan took it for a test drive. It was perfect. (Well, almost, it didn't have a flat-bed, but that didn't matter. It was just what I wanted. God had found me the perfect truck.) I told the guy that I would take the truck. He needed to get all his stuff out of it and a fuel tank off the back, so I told him that I would pick it up the next day. (That would also let the check clear the bank that we just deposited two hours before.)

We were all still standing there talking, (My wife says that I talk too much.) when my phone rang. I didn't want to answer it right then, but because it looked like a long distance number, I decided to. It was the old man that had bought my Ford. He started out by saying that he wanted to call me and tell me how blessed that I was. The reason that I was blessed was that the truck I sold him "came all to pieces" with his son and two daughters and it could have happened with me and if I had been driving fast, I could have been killed or I could have killed somebody. He went on to tell me that as his son and two granddaughters got back into Clanton, yesterday, after leaving my house, that the truck got to where his son could not control it any more. He said that the "whole front end fell out from under the truck; that it came all to pieces." His son and two granddaughters were not hurt but if I had been driving I could have been killed, because I probably drive faster than his son. So he wanted to tell me how blessed I must be to have not been in that truck. He also said that his son was so upset that he called him crying because it scared him so bad that he thought that he was going to hurt his daughters in the crash. They ran off the road but the son managed to keep from killing anyone. I didn't know what to say. I was at a total loss for words. All I could think of was, "I'm so sorry. I didn't know that anything was wrong with that truck. I swear I didn't think anything was wrong with it." I told him that if I had known anything was wrong, I would have fixed it before I sold it to him. He told me that they had to load the truck on a roll-back wrecker and carry it back to Sylacauga to have it repaired and he had to pick up the son and his granddaughters. I asked if he knew what all was wrong with it and he said something about the whole A-frame dropped out and that the ball joints broke and that it ruined one of the tires. I asked if he knew how much it was going to cost for the parts and I would send him a check. He told me that it was around a thousand dollars now, but that they were going to have to put the front end back together before they would know what all else got tore up when all that stuff came a loose. I told him once again how sorry I was that it happened and that I would make it right. (A terrible feeling came over me that he may tell me that since the truck tore up, that he had changed his mind and that I may have to end up buying the truck back. Things were going so well and now it seemed that everything had hit a brick wall.)

I got off the phone and tried to explain what had happened to Stan and the guy that I had just bought the truck from. They had heard my end of the conversation and both of them were standing there, not really knowing what to say. (I almost told the guy that I couldn't buy his truck, due to the new developments, but I decided to hang with it because I really felt that this was the truck that I was supposed to have. But, I was still really worried.)

The fellow told me that he would try and get the truck cleaned out that night and have his wife find the title. He was going to call me the next morning (Thursday) when he was finished and I could come pick it up.

That night was worse than the night before. I didn't hardly sleep at all. All I could do was to think about if the old guy didn't want my truck now and how I was going to buy it back, seeing how I had just bought another one. I also just could not figure out how all that "stuff" could have fallen out from under my other truck. I knew that it pulled a little to the right, but I had no idea that it could have been something that bad; surely I should have felt or heard something. And I could not figure what he was talking about when he said the A-frame fell out. I've worked on a bunch of trucks, and to the best of my knowledge, there is no A-frame under that Ford.

The next morning arrived way too soon for me, but I got up and tried to figure out what to do if I had to buy that Ford back. I finally decided that I would just borrow the money. (That meant that I wouldn't have to make a payment for a whole year if I put it on a yearly note.) Surely I could find someone to buy one of the trucks within a year; at least I hoped that I could.

Around nine o'clock, Mr. Chisholm called me and said that the truck was ready. He also wanted to see if I would advise him on some food plots that he wanted to plant for his daughter. He even wanted to know how much I charged for my services. I told him that any advice I had would be free. He wanted to know, though, because he knew some folks, doctors I think, that owned a hunting club that may need my services. (This was turning out better than I thought. I still hadn't made it to Scottsboro, but I may still get a job consulting.)

Before I left, something told me to go to Sylacauga and check on my Ford. So I told my wife that I was going to talk to the old man and check on what all had fell off my truck. She asked me if I was going to take my new truck up there or drive her car. She said that it probably wouldn't look good if I came driving up in a new truck just two days after selling him one that tore up. It might look as though I had known my other one was going to tear up and that I had already had a replacement in mind. I informed her that I had told the old man that I was going to have to get me something pretty quick because he had bought my only truck; so he should expect me to be in a new truck. I also told her that the guy said that the Dodge got between nineteen and twenty miles per gallon; so I could drive it.

Irene and Lindsey have to go to town every Thursday for Lindsey's piano lesson. Since piano wasn't until two o'clock that afternoon, Irene decided that if I wanted to leave early, that she would take me to get my truck. We would drop Lindsey off at Irene's mom and dad's while we went to get the truck and then, she would come back, get Lindsey, eat lunch and then take Lindsey to piano.

While she was doing that, I would leave straight from Slapout and drive to Harpersville and talk to the old man and then go to Sylacauga and check on my Ford.

Jessica did not want to go to town and wanted to just stay at the house by herself and finish school. (We home school.) I talked her into going with us (Well, I kinda told her that she had to go.) to see my new truck and that she could ride with me to Harpersville. (I don't really know why I wanted Jessica to go with me; but I thought that it would be better if she went. With all the things that had been going on, it would be nice for her to keep me company.)

After dropping off Lindsey with her grandmother, (Lindsey didn't mind being dropped off because they were going to pick up a new puppy. The puppy beat out seeing my new truck.) we headed to get my new truck. We arrived at the guy's frame and body shop and both Irene and Jessica gave their approval of my new truck. While they patiently waited, me and the guy talked for I don't know how long (Irene says that I talk too much.) about deer and turkey hunting and what to plant for his food plots and about the folks that may want me to help them with their hunting club. We also discussed my Ford truck and what possibly could have happened to it. We never reached any type conclusion because neither of us could figure how something like that could have happened.

I finally wrote the guy a check and me and Jessica loaded up to head to Harpersville. We pulled out of his yard and started out the little dirt road that led to the main road. (Which really wasn't that biga' road either.) Just before we got out to the "black top", we caught up with Irene. She had stopped in the middle of the dirt road and was getting out of the car. She came walking back to my truck with something in her hand; it was her GPS that I had given her a few years ago. (It stays in her car because I never get to go anywhere in my truck. You know, because it got terrible fuel mileage. My idea is that my wife just liked driving my truck while I was gone. She never cared if I went anywhere, just as long as I took her car, but then when I would get home, I would find out that she had been all over in my truck. Go figure.) She handed me the GPS where I would be able to find my way back to Harpersville. (I had just been there two days prior. Surely I could find my way back. I know that I don't get to go many places, but I pay real close attention when I get to.) I explained to her that I thought that I could find my way back, but she said that it would help me find the body shop in Sylacauga. (That probably was smart because I had no clue where Sylacauga was.) I then broke the news to her that my new truck was equipped with on board navigation. (How cool is that; I've never even had a vehicle with that on it.) She made me take her GPS anyway. (This still was probably a good idea, because I didn't have an inkling of how to work the one in the truck.) I thanked her for her wisdom and me and Jessica drove away.

The guy that I bought the truck from had told me how to get to the interstate by going a different way that I had come and I was going to try it because it was supposedly a lot quicker. We headed down this little curvy road and it started raining. I finally figured how to get the windshield wipers to work like I wanted them to, when I heard Jessica say, "Don't hit the deer!" I looked up and saw a big ol' doe run across the road about sixty yards ahead of me. (It was peculiar that a deer would be crossing the road at twelve forty-five in the middle of the day, especially seeing how it was so warm. In my professional deer guiding capacity, I would have thought she would have been laying up some where.) I told Jessica that I was not going to hit the deer. (I think my exact words were, "I ain't gona' hit that deer.) The deer ran all the way across the road and disappeared in the woods on the far side. I was just fixin' to ask Jessica why she wanted to holler and scare me about that deer when something slammed into the driver's side of my new truck. WHAM (Just in case you were wondering, I capitalized wham because it was really loud.) I looked in my left side mirror just in time to see another big ol' doe banging all down the side of the truck and tumbling into the air with what looked like about half of my driver's side fender that used to cover the dual wheels. I slammed on the brakes as I heard Jessica say, "O MY GOSH!" (You know why I capitalized that.) The truck came to a jerking stop as I remembered that this was a stick-shift and I had forgotten to push the clutch, although I did get it pushed prior to the truck choking down. The deer, which I could still see in my side mirror, got up, regained her composure and went running up the bank on the other side of the road, her back leg swinging behind her. My daughter's next words were, "Dang, we don't have a gun to kill the thing with!" (Spoken like a true Southern Bell.)

The second deer had evidently jumped off the bank and tried to jump over my truck. (Although that would have been a good plan, I don't think she quite figured it right.) She slammed into the back door, hit the back of the cab and bounced all the way down the side of the bed, leaving dents everywhere she hit. Although the door and the cab were not too terrible, the bed was pretty torn up.

I just sat there in the middle of the road, not really knowing what to do or say. I had owned my new truck for almost all of eight minutes now and had already torn it up. I glanced in the side mirror again and could see part of my "used to be fender" laying in the road behind the truck. I told Jessica that I was going to get it. (She thought that I was going to track down the deer and kill it with a stick or something; so she was somewhat surprised when I returned carrying a four foot piece of fiberglass.) As I threw the broken fender into the bed of the truck, the thought occurred to me that I didn't have any insurance on this truck. (OH MY GOSH, WHAT ELSE COULD GO WRONG! I wasn't speaking out loud, but I was thinking really loud. At least it was really loud when I heard me think it.) I climbed back in the truck and sat down. Jessica said, "I thought you were going to look for the deer." The only word that I could muster was, "No." (Right about this time, I kinda started to feel a little sorry for myself. This whole deal with selling and buying a truck had just been terrible. I really just wanted to sit there in the road and cry. I thought all this was going to work out perfect and that this was the truck that God wanted for me. I must have been just slap-ka-dab wrong. I felt awful, and I still had to go tell the old man how sorry I was about selling him the pitiful truck that fell all to pieces and almost killed everybody. OH MY GOSH, WHAT A TERRIBLE DAY!)

Me and Jessica headed on down the road, reliving the accident at least twelve times within the next five miles. As we drove, I constantly made Jessica look back into the bed of the truck to make sure that the four foot piece of fiberglass was still there. I could just see it flying out of the truck and hitting someone's windshield. (With how my day was going, that was a distinct possibility. I wished a million times that I had not even picked it up out of the road.)

I called the guy I purchased the truck from to tell him the good news about his "baby", as he called it when he told me about his truck and see if he knew of a good body shop. (You know I was kinda kidding because he owns a body shop. I'm sure he could tell by my voice that my day was going pretty bad and I think that he even felt a little sorry for me too.) I made plans to stop back by his shop on my way back from Sylacauga.

I finally got up with my insurance lady, after calling twice while they were out to lunch, and she thought I was kidding when I told her that I wanted to insure a new truck and file a claim on it at the same time. After a lot of explaining, she informed me that it would take some doing, but that she didn't see a problem with it. (I was really glad.) Jessica read her the VIN number and all the other particulars about the truck as I drove toward Harpersville. (I kept thinking, man, if I had just gone back to the interstate the other way, none of this would have happened.)

As we got closer to Harpersville, I was thinking about what I was going to say to the old man. I really didn't know what to say, except that I was truly sorry and that I really didn't know that anything was wrong with that truck. Man, I hated to have to talk to him. (Mainly because I know that if someone sold me a truck that tore all to pieces the same day, I would swear that they knew something was wrong with it when they sold it to me. I figured that he probably thought the same thing.) I decided that I would call the old man and tell him that I was on my way and that I was coming to make it right. (I had put a blank check in my pocket before I left the house.) He told me that there was no reason for me to come all that way because the parts were not in. After they came in and were put on, then they would know a lot more about what all was wrong. I shouldn't worry about coming all that way. He would save me the tore up parts to see after they got it all put back together. I told him that I was already almost there and that I would see him in a few minutes. (I had a funny feeling after I hung up the phone. Seemed like he would want me to see what all had happened.)

We pulled into the fruit stand and the old guy was standing there, just like the first time: pants, a tee shirt and with a hand-towel stuck down the neck of the shirt to wipe his face with. I got out and said "Hello". Jessica decided that she would just sit in the truck. I started out by reiterating how sorry I was about the truck and started asking about some of the particulars. He got to telling me about what all had happened but some of it just didn't make any sense to me. I still couldn't understand what exactly fell out from under the truck. I finally asked him, "Well, where is the truck now?" He told me that he really didn't know. I said, "Well is it at the body shop?" He said, "No I think they took it to the owner of the shop's house." He told me that his son was doing some plumbing work for Mr. Oglethorpe, the shop owner, and that he thought that they probably carried it up there, but that they were going to take it back to the shop to work on it. (I figured that they were going to work out some kind of swap, plumbing work for fixing the truck, and that he didn't want me to know about that.) I asked him how far it was to this Mr. Oglethorpe's house. He pointed in a general direction and said that he didn't really know, but it was at least twenty miles. My next question was, "Why did they take it to Mr. Oglethorpe's house to start with?" (I was thinking that maybe Mr. Oglethorpe drove the roll-back straight to his house because it was so late when he got back from picking up the truck.) He told me that his son carried it up there. I asked, "Is it still on the roll-back?" He said that it wasn't on the roll-back, and that his son carried it up there because he was doing some work up there. (This wasn't making any sense to me.)

"Did he drive it up there?" I asked. "Yeah, he drove it. (I'm fixin' to quit writing all this "I said" and "He said" stuff. I'm just going to write what we said; I'm sure yall can figure out who said what.) "Well, I thought you said that it fell all to pieces; how did he drive it?" "Well, they just stuck it back together and told him to drive it easy, but there ain't no use in going up there to look at it. The parts will be in sometime this afternoon, around two or three o'clock and they're going to bring it back to the shop to fix it, then we'll know what all else got tore up." "Thought you said that all the parts fell out from under the truck? How did they put them back?" "Well, you know them ball joints will pop in and out." (NO THEY WON'T! I'm getting a really weird feeling about all this.) "So, well, they put it back; they popped them back in." "Well where did they put it when they unloaded it off the roll-back, at the shop or at the guy's house?" "Well, no they didn't bring it on the roll-back." "I thought you said that they had to put it on a roll-back to get it home because everything fell out from under it." "Well, I thought that they did. I told my son that he had my VISA card so he could just load it up on a roll-back and bring it home but he decided to drive it, but he had to go really slow. It took him till about ten thirty or eleven o'clock to get home cause he had to drive so slow." (I'm now completely lost and am getting a little agitated with the old man, well maybe more than a little agitated.) "So he drove the truck home?" "Yeah, he drove it home but had to go really slow." "So did anything fall out from under the truck?" "Well, no, but he said it sounded like it did and when he got out to see, that's when he found out what all had come apart." "So he's still driving the truck and he didn't wreck! I thought that you told me that they wrecked!" "Well at the time, I thought he had." "OK, look, when are the parts arriving?" "This afternoon, but there's no reason for you to hang around that long." "Are the parts coming in to Oglethorpe's?" "Yeah, around three o'clock or so."

Thank goodness, about that time, some guy pulled up in a van to buy some tomatoes. (I was about ready to bust. I didn't know what this old guy was doing, but I didn't like the way it was going. I had a real bad feeling.) The fellow got out and proceeded to get his tomatoes as I was opening my door to head to Oglethorpe's. As I got the door open, there sat Jessica. I had kinda forgotten she was still in the truck. I introduced her to the old guy. (I'd like to call him something different about now but I don't know who all may read this.) After Jessica got to tell the old guy "Hello", the other fellow walked up with his bag of tomatoes and started to talk to the old guy. I was fixin' to interrupt their conversation and say "Bye", when the tomato guy (We'll just call him that.) started talking to me too. He asked me how long I had known the old guy. I told him only a couple of days. He proceeded to tell me how long he had known him and what a tough old man he was and that everyone thought that he should have died when he got run over and then when he got cancer, but that he hadn't and that it must have been a miracle of God. I told him "Yeah, from what I had heard, it sure sounded like it." He went on to tell me of what a good Christian man the old guy was and that God must have had a reason for him to have stayed on this earth. As the tomato guy started to leave, the old man invited him to come go to church with him next Sunday.

Even though I had been settled down somewhat by the tomato guy, I still had a bad feeling about the story that the old man had told me. It looked to me like I was being had. (I ain't never been real keen on being had.)

Me and Jessica headed down the road toward Oglethorpe's Garage that was in Sylacauga. As we rode, I started to discuss with Jessica my feelings about the old man's story, and how it just really didn't add up. (I was amazed at how much of the conversation between me and the old man Jessica could repeat back to me, almost word for word. I'll have to make a mental note of that for when I have any other, what I consider, semi-private conversations close to the truck.)

About half way, according to Irene's GPS, to Oglethorpe's, I called my buddy Stan and discussed what the old man had said. Stan told me that he would have never gone up there to start with and that I should come on home and forget about the whole thing. I told him that I felt bad about the truck, but now I don't even know what, if anything, really happened, but that I hoped that this Mr. Oglethorpe may be able to shed some light on the subject.

After hanging up with Stan, I decided that the best thing to do now was to try and calm down; so me and Jessica decided to stop at Taco Bell and eat lunch. (I know that I always said that I call my mid-day meal dinner, but I will sometimes call it lunch, because when you eat at Taco Bell, it's really not like sitting down and eating a "meal." It's just getting some food.) While sitting there at Taco Bell, I went over the conversation that I had with the old man a couple more times (probably twenty) to see if I could make heads or tails of it. No matter how I tried, I just couldn't make all his claims fit. The stories just didn't add up. (I don't know if the son ever lost control of the truck. I don't know if anything ever really fell off the truck. And, I don't know if anything is even wrong with it at all. Surely the old man would not have made all this up!) We finished our food and headed on down the road to see if Mr. Oglethorpe could help me make some sense of this fiasco.

As we pulled into the shop, I read the sign that said, Oglethorpe's Transmission Repair. (I thought it was kinda odd that my truck would have been carried to a transmission shop.) An older, grey-haired man with a beard had just come out of the shop walking behind a lady. I just kinda stood there, not wanting to interrupt their conversation. The lady finally started getting in her car to leave and the fellow asked me if he could help me. I asked him if he was Mr. Oglethorpe and he said, "Yes". I told him who I was and explained to him that I was the guy that had owned the red Ford 450 prior to it falling apart. I asked him about what all was wrong with it, and to my surprise, he acted like he didn't know what I was talking about. (Imagine that!) I explained to him that it was the one that the guy working on his plumbing was driving and that I knew about the deal that they were working, about swapping out some plumbing work for the price of fixing the truck. He just looked at me, really puzzled like, and told me that he didn't know the old man that I was talking about and that he didn't have anybody working on his house. He also told me that they were a transmission shop and that they really didn't do that type of work in the first place. Around about then, I almost passed out. I was so upset that I had forgotten to breathe. I was sooo mad that I didn't even know what to do. The first thing that came to mind was to go back, take the cane from the old man and beat him with it. (I told you that I wasn't the best Christian.)

I got back in the truck and told Jessica, "He lied, he lied, that old man lied to me! This guy doesn't know anything about my truck. (I imagine that Jessica had already heard my conversation, but I wanted to tell someone.) He made the whole thing up! Ain't nothing wrong with my truck! That old man lied just to get me to send him some money." I was so mad that I was shaking. I wanted to go back up to that fruit stand so bad that I didn't know what to do. All I could think about, though, was that there sat Jessica. There was no way that I could go up there and say what I wanted to say (And say it the way that I wanted to say it.) with her in the truck. I really didn't want her to see me act and talk like that.

I finally just decided to pull off the road and sit and think about it for a while. While sitting there, I thought about going by and seeing if I could find his son. I figured that I could remember how to get to the barn that we picked him up at two days before. Then I remembered that he had called me right after leaving my house the other day because he had made a wrong turn. Surely I could find his cell phone number on my phone. I started looking, almost franticly, because my cell phone was steady vibrating, telling me that my battery was low. I finally decided on what number must have been his, based on the time line. (And after seeing all the calls that I had received and made in the last two days, I decided that my wife may be right. I do talk too much.)

I didn't have a phone charger with me, and I could see my phone going dead right in the middle of me fussin' at the son, (You loose a lot of your steam when you have to call someone back when your fussin' at them.) so I asked Jessica if I could borrow hers'. (I was real glad that she had come about now.) She handed me her phone and I called the son. All I got was his answering machine, but that was a good thing because it told me his name and I had forgotten it. I started leaving him a message to call me back and about how important that it was, when, right as I was leaving him my phone number, that I remembered that I was on Jessica's phone.

Well, when I call Jessica, all I do is scroll down to her name in the contact list and push "Send". I don't have a clue what her phone number is. So right in the middle of my "so called" very important message, I almost locked up. I quickly looked to Jessica to help bale me out by giving me her phone number, and almost instantaneously found out that Jessica has never called herself and that she was not sure of her number either. Seeing how much time I had before I exploded, Jessica came up with the number to her phone. I rattled it off to the son, just like I had known it forever and told him that I would be waiting for his call, sitting on the side of the road in Sylacauga.

Terribly flustered but still functioning, I handed Jessica her phone back and tried to apologize for hollering and told her "Thank You" for letting me use her phone. (I was really glad that she was there.) As I was doing this, she broke the news to me that she was pretty sure that the phone number she had given me was, in fact, Lindsey's. (I hollered at poor Jessica again. For some reason, I felt as though I needed to explain to her that the phone number was of utmost importance and that since she gave me the wrong one, the whole world was about to end. Bless her heart, she probably wished she had not come with me.) Me and her finally got it all settled and I had to ask to borrow her phone again. (I bet she thought about throwing it out the window.)

I called the son the second time and to my surprise, he answered. I started out by asking him if he had wrecked on the way home from my house. He said, "No". I tried to calmly (But, during my whole conversation, Jessica kept telling me to stop hollering.) explain to him what his father had told me and that I had come up to Harpersville to make it right. I also told him about the fact that if the old man had not lied to me, that I would not have had my new truck torn up by the deer. He apologized and told me that he didn't know why his father would have told me that. He also went on to say that the truck did fine all the way home, but that when he turned into his driveway, he heard a pop. After getting to the house he checked and said that he found that the passenger's side tie rod end was bad. That was all that he knew was wrong with the truck; none of the other stuff had happened. He had talked to his dad about that before his dad had called me. (So the old man knew the whole story about the truck before he called and made up that flamboyant lie. He didn't want to tell me about how blessed I was; he wanted to trick me into paying for the new tie rod end, and anything else he might find wrong. The tomato guy must have been mistaken about the old man being such a Christian. His actions sure didn't make him seem that way.)

I informed the son that I was not going (could not go) to see the old man; and that even though I had come up there to make things right, that I was through with them and that I didn't care what all may or may not be wrong with the truck, "I was going home". He said that he understood, apologized once again and said that he would have a talk with his father.

As we headed back to the frame and body shop, poor Jessica had to hear the whole story, I imagine, twenty more times. I also had to borrow her phone a couple more times to call Irene and my buddy Stan to tell them the "rest of the story". I was so mad! How could anyone do me like that! I had been lied to and had got my new truck torn up. But, Thank God, I had gone up there to check, or I would have gladly sent him some money, probably several thousand, to fix the truck; because I felt horrible for selling him that "death trap".

# III-MY EYES OPENED

When you are driving, you have plenty of time to think of wild ideas and deep thoughts; so I tried to make some sense of what had happened in the last couple of days. I was really sure that God had answered my prayer of helping me to find the right truck. I just could not believe that He had given me the perfect truck and that that old man, by lying to me, had caused me to get it torn up. How in the world could God have let this happen. What was He trying to tell me? I decided that maybe the lesson for me was that God gives us things, but He can take them away just as fast. I didn't have any idea; I just knew that I was still mad with the old man, but that maybe God sent me up there to keep me from wasting my money.

I was really embarrassed when I pulled up to the frame and body shop. I hated to let the guy see his truck that he thought so much of and that I had torn up so quickly. (I figured that he probably wished that he hadn't sold it to me.) I started out my conversation with him by telling him that it was the old man's fault, because if he hadn't lied to me, I would not have gone that way and my truck (his truck) would have never been damaged.

The first thing that he said was "Well, you said that you wanted a flat bed. The money for the estimate will probably almost pay for the one that you wanted." (The bed that I wanted was around five thousand dollars installed. I had sold my Ford for twenty-five thousand, paid twenty-three thousand for this truck, and with the three thousand dollar estimate check from the insurance; my new bed would be paid for. O Happy Day!) I COULD NOT BELIEVE IT. GOD HAD GIVEN ME THE TRUCK I WANTED AND THE NEW BED TO GO WITH IT. THANK YOU LORD!

As Jessica and I drove home, I was overwhelmed with thoughts of all kinds. I tried to tie all the circumstances of the last two or three days together and figure out how they could have happened like they did. There was no way that everything could have worked out the way it did without God's help. He had not just helped me to find a truck; He had gotten me the truck, just like I wanted. I hadn't helped a bit. (I was soo thankful! I couldn't fathom why I received such a great blessing, knowing that I surely didn't deserve it. My whole life I have been blessed with everything that I ever needed and probably almost everything I ever wanted. God has preformed miracles in my life from the time I was born, but I have never really seen them for what they were until recently. I was just amazed sometimes how things just seemed to work out. I really didn't give credit to God, but I should have. He had now opened my eyes.)

Let me try and tie all the things together and show you what I mean.

To start with, I know, beyond a shadow of a doubt that God told me to call Buddy.

If the guy's injector hadn't blown out and busted the piston, he never would have taken it to the shop.

If he hadn't taken it to the shop, Buddy would not have known about the truck.

If the engine hadn't torn up, he also would have never put the new clutch in it.

The truck was out of warranty, but Dodge paid for the engine, even though nobody ever thought that they would.

The guy never sold the truck, even though he had wanted to; he had never even advertised it. It was like he was saving it for me, whether he knew it or not.

He also talked to me about a possible consulting job. You remember that the reason that the old guy didn't come see my truck sooner was because I told him that I would stop by there on my way to Scottsboro to talk to a fellow about a consulting job.

Two separate people wanted to buy my Ford truck, but for some unknown reason they never called back, even though the banks should have given them the money, because I was asking well below loan.

If my bank stock had not plummeted, I would have never got the blood test to get additional insurance and they would have never thought that I had prostate cancer.

If I had never been told that I may have had cancer, and the old man had never had prostate cancer, I would have never taken it as a "sign" to go and talk to the old man.

I would have had him come and see my truck at my house, and then I would have never got his son's phone number.

The old man was run over by a semi-tractor truck and even though no one thought that he would live, he did. He told me that he thought that he must have been left for a reason.

The old guy decided to buy my truck, even though he didn't need it.

If we hadn't had so much trouble at the credit union, the mileage issue would have never come up and I would have sold the truck for twenty-six thousand; just like we had agreed.

Since the mileage issue did come up, I was pretty much forced to sell the truck for twenty-five thousand.

That left the two thousand dollars difference between the prices of the trucks, even though I thought I had sold the Ford too cheap.

If the old guy had not lied to me, I would have never gone to check on my Ford truck in Sylacauga.

If I had not gone to check on it, the deer would not have hit my truck.

If the body shop guy had not told me to go that way, the deer would have not hit my truck.

If Irene hadn't stopped me in the road, I would have gone down the road before the deer got there.

All these things came together to make it possible for me to get the one truck that I really needed. (Well, not really needed, but really wanted.) It was the perfect truck that gets great fuel mileage, has a brand new motor and clutch, a brand new bed that I got for free, a big bumper and winch, a limited slip differential, on board navigation, and all the bells and whistles that I could think of. THANK YOU LORD!

I'm not even mad with the old man any more because I know that he was just carrying out the will of God. I know now that is why the tomato guy came by during our conversation and told me what a good Christian man the old guy was. (I guess that's why the Bible tells us not to judge. I really had the wrong idea about the old guy. Even though it looked terrible to me, the old guy was doing exactly what God wanted him to do.)

You know, during this whole ordeal, and after it was over, I thought that this was all just for me. Man, God has blessed me with this new truck. I was so appreciative and to show my appreciation to God, I wanted to tell people what He had done for me. I told my wife, my mom, my buddy Stan and even called another friend of mine, Bobby, to tell him what God had done for me.

I had sometimes told people about how things miraculously just worked out for me but I had never really given the credit to God. I had said, "Just by the grace of God", or something like that, but never really said that God did it. This time, I really said it.

A few days after my ordeal was over, I went to town to file the title application and pay for the taxes and title fee. While I was at the title office, for some reason the girl in the window asked me if I had gotten rid of that Ford that I was trying to sell. (I still don't know how she knew that I was trying to sell it.) I told her that I had and even though it was a line behind me, I felt compelled to tell her the story. I really don't know why, but I felt better after I did; and I really kinda hoped that some of the folks in the line heard me too.

Before I left for town, I decided that while I was over there, I would try and go by and get me a hair cut. I had been trying to get my hair, or what's left of it, cut for about two weeks. (My hair is not turning grey, it's turning loose. I'm almost positive that I'm gona' be bald headed in just a few years. I don't like it worth a flip.) Every time that I had called, Teresa, the lady that cuts my hair, (I don't know if you are supposed to call a lady a barber or not.) she was always out. (She's never out.) So, I called before I got there, just to make sure. And sure enough, this time she was working.

I walked in and just like most times, people were ahead of me. I sat down and got situated, because usually it's quite a while before she gets to me. (It's only two ladies that work in the barber shop and each of us has "our barber" and will only get our hair cut by that one, even though the other one would probably do just as good a job.)

Most people that come into the barber shop always say "Hello" to the "barbers" but most of the time, you just sit quietly, look around, look at a magazine, (Although lately, they have more "women's stuff" magazines and less hunting magazines.) or some guys even take them a short nap. I have tried all the above except for the nap. (You never know if you may make some type weird noise or something and when you wake up, everyone would be staring at you.)

After I had been there for about twenty minutes, an older gentleman came in and sat down one chair over from me. I nodded to him "Hello", as most people do when you are not really going to talk out loud, and continued my blank stare toward the far wall. To my surprise, the older guy started talking to me. I don't remember exactly how he started the conversation, but it just kept going. He was talking about weird stuff to be talking about in the barber shop. (You're supposed to talk, if you talk, about hunting or the weather or maybe about sports or something.) He was talking about where we came from and how some people thought that we came from monkeys (I stopped him there and told him that I was sure that I didn't come from a monkey.) and getting real close to talking about God. (It has always kinda made me uncomfortable to talk about God in public unless it's some type of religious function. I was always OK with that, I guess, because everyone else was talking about Him.) He went on to tell me about his brother and that his brother had some illness (I think cancer, but I'm not sure.) and that he was going to die any time now. They had called Hospice in and that it would not be long. I explained to him that I thought that sometimes that it is better for you to know when it is near and you have time to get yourself right with your maker. (At that very moment I felt funny that I had not said God. Something told me that I should have.) And, that it makes it easier on the family because they expect it and may even be glad that the person did not have to suffer any longer. It's always terrible on the family if someone dies unexpectedly. It leaves a huge void that is never really filled, an empty feeling that they are gone and that you may have neglected to do something for them or say something to them and that you never will get the chance. (My father died when I was nine months old, so I never really knew him. So, when my mother remarried when I was five, my stepfather became my only real father that I had ever known. He treated me just like his own son and I considered him to be my father. I'm reminded of him every time I hear that song about the fellow that was the "dad he didn't have to be". The child in the song was so proud that the guy took his mom out on a date and he got to go too. Bo, my step father, did the same thing for me. His real name was Robert, but some people called him: Bobby, Bo, or Bo Bo, depending on what time in his life they had known him. Even though I was only five, I still remember that I almost always got to go with him and Mama. He liked to take us to "The Embers" in Montgomery, and I would always get veal cutlet. Bo died after a long struggle and Hospice was called in, just like the older gentleman's brother, so we all knew that he would not be around very long. I had never really remembered telling Bo that I loved him. Because of the long illness and the fact that we knew he was going to die soon, I had the opportunity to tell him that I loved him and that I was proud of him. Since my "real" dad died when I was really young, I have always hoped that if he can see me or know about me, that I have lived my life in a way that would have made him proud. I always wanted Bo to know that I was proud of him as well. I will treasure that moment for the rest of my life and I thank God that He gave me the chance. If Bo had died unexpectedly, I would have worried about not telling him forever.) So, I told him that it was what I thought, a blessing, even if it was hard on the person that had to suffer.

He then got to talking about some people think that you go to heaven and some people think that you don't. (Man, I really didn't want to talk about this in the barber shop.) I just sat there and let him talk, not really knowing what to say or if he wanted me to speak at all. He then told me that he heard that it said in the Bible that everyone had a purpose and that everyone had a talent, but that he had never found his talent and that he had lived his whole life and didn't think that he had ever had a purpose. I really didn't know what to say, so I said, "Well, you know, sometimes your purpose may just to be somewhere on a certain day and time to keep someone from doing something or just to happen to be in someone's way that keeps them from getting in an accident or something". (I was really grabbing at straws. I really didn't want to have this conversation, especially in the barber shop.)

All of a sudden something told me, "Tell him your story." I started in on my story, knowing that I probably didn't have time to finish it but I was sure that I was supposed to try. I didn't even look around to see if anyone else was listening to us. When Teresa got through with the guy in her chair, it was my turn. I did something that I had never ever thought of doing. I asked her to wait for just a few minutes until I could finish my story. She said "OK" and went on to the back. (It may have shocked her hearing me say that just as much as it did me to say it.) I finished my story as Teresa came back out from the back and told the older gentleman that, "See the old man lied to me but that was his purpose all along. He did God's will without even knowing it. He didn't know why he didn't die, but he said that he was looking for his purpose. He may have had many more, but I am sure he fulfilled one of them that day. He was an integral part of God's miracle of me getting the truck. So see, you may have been fulfilling your purpose without even knowing it."

I got up, walked over and sat down in the barber chair, feeling really good about having told the story to someone else. I hoped that it would help the gentleman feel better about his life. I wish that I had had more time to talk to him, but it must have been enough.

# IV-MY EYES REALLY OPENED

That next morning as I was laying in bed, I thanked God one more time for my new truck that he had so miraculously provided for me. That same voice that always talks to me or just pops into my head said, "It's not about you or your truck. What if all this was about having you at a certain place at a certain time? What if you got all this just to be able to tell that gentleman in the barber shop what he was supposed to hear?" I never had imagined it that way. It could have been just like I told the barber shop guy; my whole deal just led me up to being in the barber shop at that time to fulfill one of my purposes, to tell the guy about the purpose of the old man that lied. And just like the tomato guy that was there just to explain to me about the old man; to tell me what a good Christian he was, even though I thought terrible of him. And just like Irene stopping me in the road, where I wouldn't get to the deer crossing before the deer did. It goes on and on. The whole deal may have just been for the barber shop guy, not about me at all.

Then the voice came back and said, "It's not about the barber shop guy, it's about the story. God did all of this to give you the story." (OH MY GOSH! It hit me like a freight train.) The reason for all my telling was not to tell about what God did for just me and my new truck. It was not about telling the barber shop guy about his purpose. It was not about me fulfilling my purpose of being there to help the barber shop guy feel better about his life. It was about God showing me that He still does miracles every day in our lives and that if we look for them, we can see them plain as day! It was about me getting the story to tell as many people as possible about how God does miracles in our lives every day. About how they should not give up just because they may have messed stuff all up or have seemingly failed at something. The circumstances may seem overwhelming and totally impossible to them, (And it really is impossible for them alone.) but that anything is possible with God because He is really in charge of everything. If you don't believe it, just look around. God had shown me how He could make things happen by using many different people to carry out His plan without them even knowing that they were participating. He wanted me to tell the story of His everyday miracles and how He can affect our lives, even though sometimes we are totally oblivious. He can do anything, even things that we think are impossible. Even though we think things are going terrible, God may just be setting us up for something special. It's His plan not ours'. We shouldn't say that God helps us do stuff; God does it; we're just present.

I hope that everyone that reads this story will look for the miracles in their lives everyday. Even though you may think that God has forgotten about you, He may still be working one of His miracles for you, in spite of all your trying. I thought that I was making the right decisions and going to do great things. God taught me right quick that without His hand in things, I was incapable of doing anything. He showed me how powerful He really is. He can control all things. I alone can do nothing.

I thank you for reading this story. I hope that you have gotten a blessing from it; I know that I sure did. I want to leave you with one verse from the Bible that has always meant a lot to me. I hope that I and all yall can remember it and try to practice it every day.

Proverbs 3, verses 5-6
(KJV)

Trust in the Lord with all thine heart;
and lean not unto thine own understanding.
In all thy ways acknowledge him,
and he shall direct thy path.

Made in the USA
Charleston, SC
22 August 2012